# 51 things to make with Egg Cartons

**Fiona Hayes**

# Contents

## Basic Equipment

Most of these projects use some or all of the following equipment, so keep these handy:

- **White glue**
- **Scissors**
- **Pencils**
- **Ruler**
- **Felt-tip pens**
- **Paintbrushes**

Unless specified, short, six-egg cartons that have hinges on the long side are used.

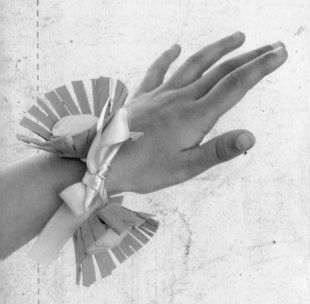

# Cute Chicken

This cute chicken is the perfect egg-holder! Make a row of these clucky cuties—they'll brighten up any kitchen.

## You will need

**One egg carton**

**White or brown paint**

**Red and yellow cardstock**

**Two googly eyes**

**1**

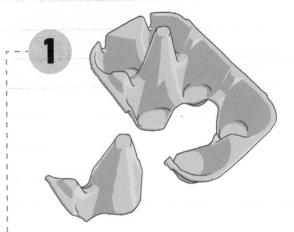

Cut the corner from the base of an egg carton. Paint your chicken white or brown.

**2**

Fold a small piece of red cardstock in half. Cut out a half-heart shape. You will need to make two of these—one for the chicken's comb and one for its wattles.

**3**

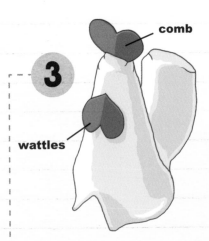

comb

wattles

Glue the comb and wattles to the body, as shown above.

**4**

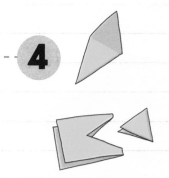

Using the same method you used in step 2, cut out a triangular beak.

**5**

Glue the beak in place. Add some googly eyes.

**6**

Why not make a row of chickens from one long egg carton? You could keep all your Easter eggs in it!

# Roaring Lion Hand Puppet

Who knew you could make a lion from an egg carton? Your friends will go WILD when they see it!

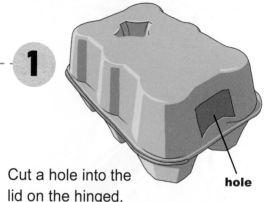

**1**

hole

Cut a hole into the lid on the hinged, short side of the egg carton. The hole should be big enough to fit two fingers inside.

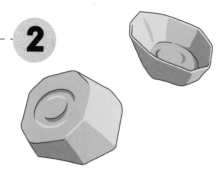

**2**

Cut two bowls from the base of another egg carton. Trim the sides to give them a sloped edge.

**3**

Glue the bowls to the top of the first carton. They will be the eyes. Paint the lion's head yellow.

**4**

Cut slits in a strip of brown felt or cardstock for the mane. You may need two pieces to make a thick mane.

**5**

Glue the mane to the head.

**6**

Cut ears from the white cardstock, paint yellow and glue into position.

**7**

Add some googly eyes.

**8**

To make your lion roar, put two fingers in the dip on its head and two fingers in the hole at the back of its head, and your thumb under the carton. Pull up the lid and hear it...

### Handy Hint

If you can't find egg cartons with hinges on the short side, cut off the lid of a regular carton and make paper hinges on the short side.

ROAR

# Bee

**Get buzzing and make a pretty bumblebee!**

## You will need

One egg carton

Yellow, black, blue, and white paint

White and blue cardstock

Two yellow bendy straws

Two googly eyes

**1** Paint the top of your carton yellow and the bottom black. Add black stripes to the top.

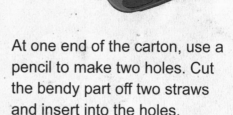

**2** At one end of the carton, use a pencil to make two holes. Cut the bendy part off two straws and insert into the holes.

**3** Cut out two wings from white cardstock. Paint veins on the wings, then glue into position. Paint a mouth onto your bee.

**4** Add blue circles of cardstock behind the eyes to make them stand out. Glue the eyes to the blue circles and then to the egg carton. Buzz, buzz, your bee is ready!

# Hedgehog

This hedgehog is so adorable all your friends will want to make one.

**1**

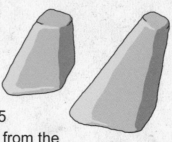

Cut out 12–15 pointed parts from the bottom of an egg carton. Trim the bottoms so they are slightly angled.

**2**

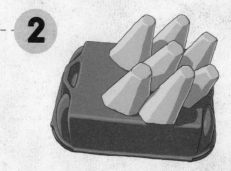

Glue the parts onto one end of an egg carton. Allow the parts on the top to dry before you glue parts to the sides.

**3**

Once the glue is dry, paint the top of the body and spikes brown, and the rest yellow.

**4**

Cut a bowl from the base of an egg carton, paint it yellow. Glue it to the head, to make a snout. Use a bottle top for the nose. Glue it to the snout. Add circles of felt, then add the eyes. Your hedgehog is now ready to sniff around!

# Barking Dog Hand Puppet

## You will need

**Two egg cartons**
(one must have hinges on the short side)

**Brown, black, and red paint**

**Brown and black felt**

**Two googly eyes**

**1**

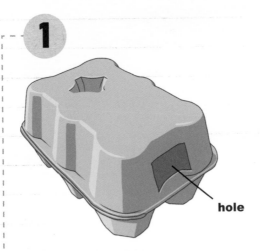

hole

Cut a hole into the lid on the hinged, short side of the egg carton. The hole should be big enough to fit two fingers inside.

**2**

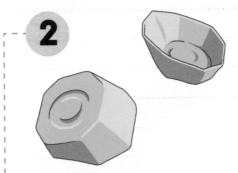

Cut two bowls from the base of another carton. Trim the sides to give them a sloped edge.

**3**

Glue the bowls to the top of the carton. They will be the dog's eyes.

**4**

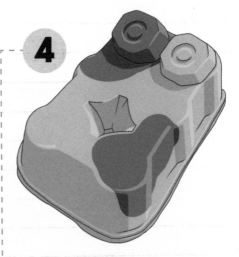

Now paint your dog. Don't forget to paint the inside of its mouth red!

**5**

Cut a pair of ears and
a nose from felt.

**6**

Glue in place.

**7**

Add some googly eyes.

**8**

To make your dog bark, put two fingers
in the dip on its head, two fingers in the
hole at the back of its head, and your
thumb under the carton. Pull up the lid.

WOOF
WOOF

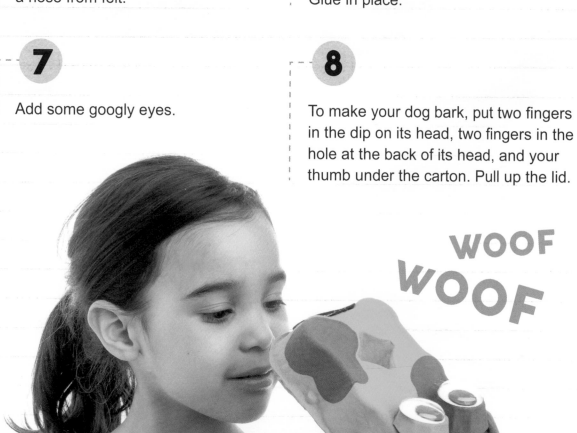

# Dragon

This red-hot dragon will fire up your egg-carton crafty collection.

### 1

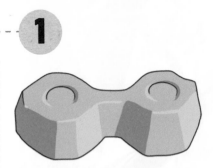

For the eyes, cut a two-bowl section from the bottom of an egg carton.

### 2

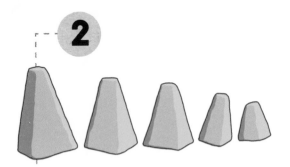

For the tail, cut six pointed parts from the bottom of another egg carton. Make the parts different sizes.

### 3

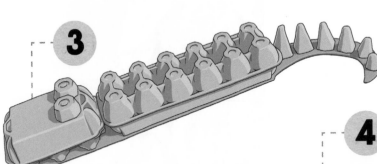

Place a short egg carton upright. Put a long egg carton alongside the short one, but upside-down. Position the tail spikes to form the tail. Now cut a piece of cardstock the same length as your dragon. Cut a curve into the cardstock, to shape the tail. Then glue all the parts onto the cardstock, as shown.

### 4

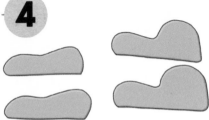

Cut out four legs from the thick cardstock and glue them onto the body, as shown in step 5.

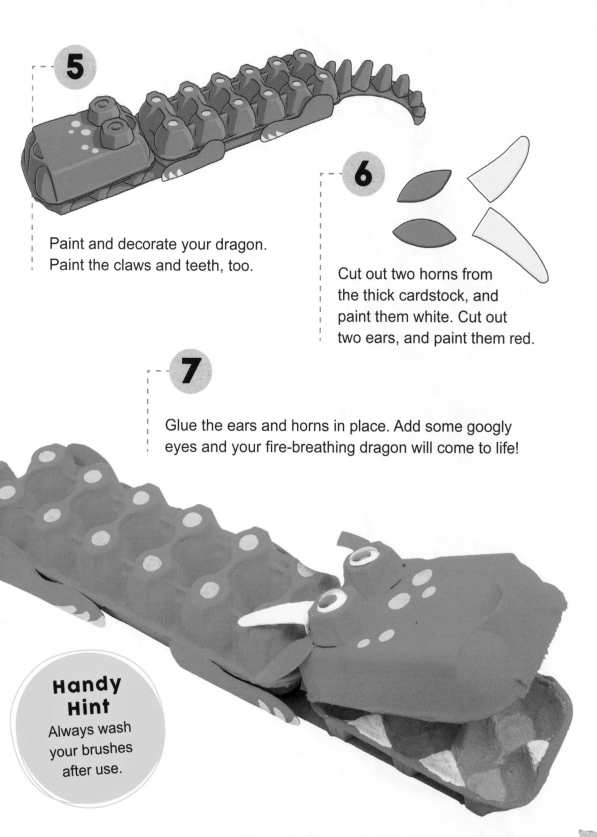

**5**

Paint and decorate your dragon. Paint the claws and teeth, too.

**6**

Cut out two horns from the thick cardstock, and paint them white. Cut out two ears, and paint them red.

**7**

Glue the ears and horns in place. Add some googly eyes and your fire-breathing dragon will come to life!

**Handy Hint**
Always wash your brushes after use.

# Dump Truck

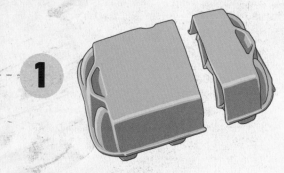

**1** Cut the small egg carton in two, as shown. The large section will be the cab.

**2** Paint the cab section. Cut out some windows from white cardstock, and draw on passengers. Glue the windows in place.

**3** Cut the lid off a long egg carton. Turn it upside-down and glue onto the egg carton base. Paint the wagon.

**4** Cut a piece of cardboard the length of the cab and wagon. Then glue them onto the cardboard.

## 5

Cut out eight circles for the wheels and paint them.

## 6

Glue the wheels onto the cab and wagon.

### Handy Hint
Use clothespins to hold pieces in place while waiting for them to dry.

## 7

Add two bottle tops to the cab, for hazard lights. Your truck is ready!

VROOM

VROOM

# Fairy Magic

Do you love fairies? You certainly will once you've made this pretty little fairy!

## You will need

**One egg carton**
**Paint**
**Yarn**
**Pink felt or cardstock**
**Foam ball**

**1**

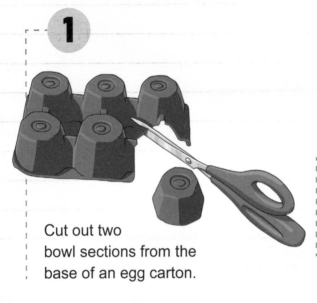

Cut out two bowl sections from the base of an egg carton.

**2**

Glue the bowls together to make a barrel.

**3**

Glue on the foam ball. Paint the ball and the bowls. For the hair, glue on some yarn.

**4**

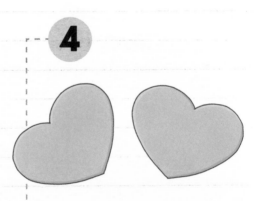

For the wings, cut out two hearts from felt or cardstock.

**5**

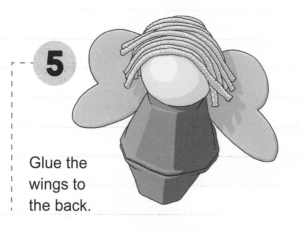

Glue the wings to the back.

**6**

Draw on some eyes and a friendly smile and your fairy is ready to wave her magic wand!

## Handy Hint

Make a few of these magical fairies so you have an entire fairy kingdom.

# Fire Engine

Save the day by making this amazing fire engine. You could make two so that you have your very own fire station!

## You will need

**Two egg cartons**

**Cardboard**

**Red, white, blue, and yellow paint**

**The tops of two toothpaste tubes**

**Three straws**

**Shiny corrugated cardstock**

**1**

Cut an egg carton in two, as shown. The large section will be the cab.

**2**

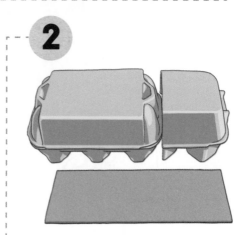

Glue the cab and another egg carton to a piece of cardboard.

**3**

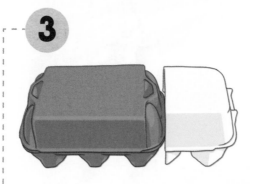

Paint the back section red, and the front part white. When the paint is dry, add some blue windows.

**4**

Cut out six circles from the thick cardstock for the wheels. Paint and glue in place. Glue two tube tops to the top of the cab.

**5**

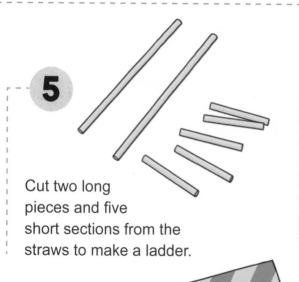

Cut two long pieces and five short sections from the straws to make a ladder.

**6**

Glue the ladder to the top of the truck.

**7**

Make a hazard sign from cardboard for the front of the truck, as shown.

**8**

Glue a piece of shiny corrugated cardstock to the truck's side. Your fire engine is ready to zoom into action!

NEE-NAW NEE-NAW

# Funny Frog

What's bright green, very cute, and will make a really big splash? This friendly little frog!

## You will need

**Two egg cartons**

**Dark green, light green, yellow, and red paint**

**Two googly eyes**

**1**

Cut two bowls from the base of an egg carton. These will be the frog's eyes.

**2**

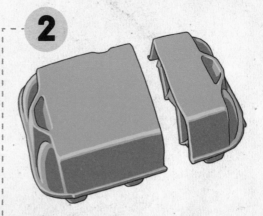

Cut the second egg carton in two, as shown. The large part will be the body.

**3**

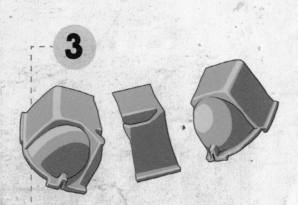

Cut the frog's legs from the lid of the small section.

**4**

Glue the frog's eyes and legs into position.

**5**

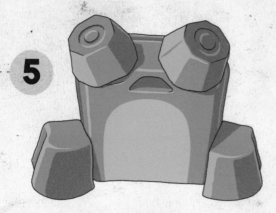

Paint the frog dark green, with a light green belly.

**Handy Hint**

Let the paint dry completely before adding the spots.

**6**

Paint on some yellow spots and a red mouth. Add googly eyes, and, boing, your frog will leap away!

RIBBIT
RIBBIT

21

# Happy Hippo

## You will need

**Three egg cartons**
**Pink and white paint**
**Cardboard**
**Two googly eyes**

**1**

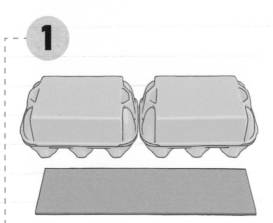

Glue two egg cartons onto a piece of cardboard.

**2**

Cut six bowls from the base of another egg carton.

**3**

Glue two bowls onto the head to make the hippo's eyes.

**4**

For the feet, glue the remaining four bowls onto the base. Paint the hippo pink.

**5**

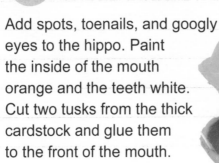

Add spots, toenails, and googly eyes to the hippo. Paint the inside of the mouth orange and the teeth white. Cut two tusks from the thick cardstock and glue them to the front of the mouth.

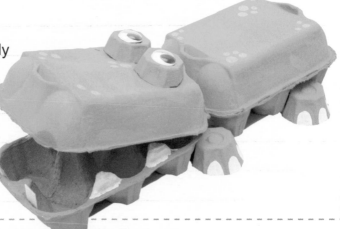

# Tortoise

## You will need

**Two egg cartons**
**Green and yellow paint**
**White cardstock**
**Two googly eyes**

**1**

Cut four bowls from the base of an egg carton.

**2**

Glue two of the bowls to the top of an upturned egg carton.

**3**

Paint the remaining two bowls yellow, then cut them in half. These will be the tortoise's feet.

**4**

Glue the feet in place.

**5**

Paint the egg carton green, with yellow circles or spots. This will be the tortoise's shell.

**6**

Cut out a circle from cardstock and paint it yellow. Glue this to the front of the shell. Add googly eyes and a smile to complete your cute little friend.

23

# Christmas Tree

It's Christmastime! Fill your house with festive cheer by making this pretty little tree.

## You will need

**Three egg cartons**

**Green, red, and yellow paint**

**Cardboard**

**Shiny cardstock**

**Ribbon**

**1**

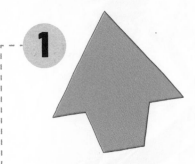

Draw a large triangle on a piece of cardboard. Add a pot shape to the bottom. Cut out.

**2**

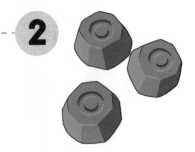

Cut 15 bowls from the base of the egg cartons.

**3**

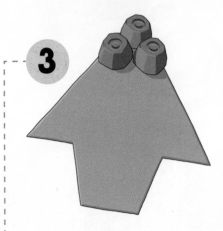

Glue the bowls to the top of the tree, so they fit together snugly.

**4**

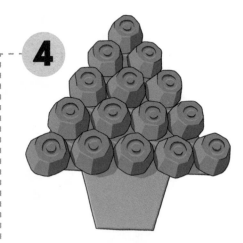

Cover the tree with bowls, but leave the pot section uncovered. Leave to dry.

**5**

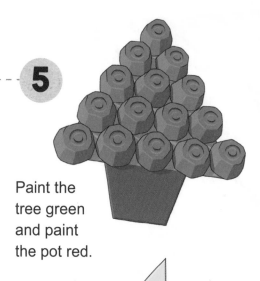

Paint the
tree green
and paint
the pot red.

**6**

Cut out lots
of circles from
shiny cardstock, to make hanging
balls. Glue them onto your tree.

**7**

Cut out a star
from thick cardstock,
and paint it yellow.

**8**

Glue the star to the top of
your tree. Attach a loop
of ribbon to the back of
the tree, so you can hang
it up at Christmastime.

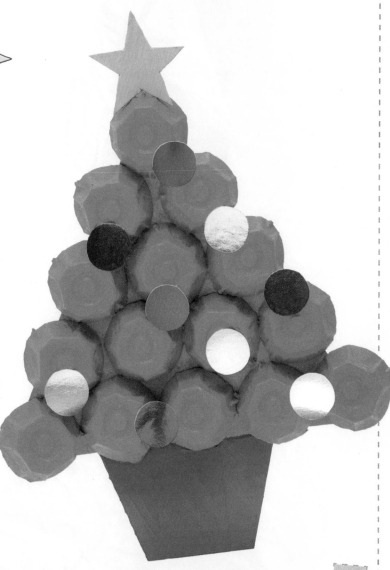

### Handy Hint
You can make this
tree as large as you
like—you just need
lots of egg
cartons!

# Snowman

Brrrr! If it's cold outside, stay indoors and make this perfect snowman—it will never melt!

## You will need

**One egg carton**
**White and black paint**
**Red felt**
**Thick orange cardstock**

**1** Cut four bowls from the base of an egg carton.

**2** Glue two bowls together, to make a barrel.

**3** Glue on another bowl, to make the head.

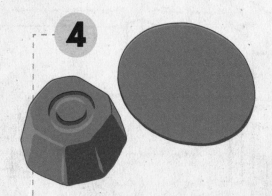

**4** Cut a circle from the lid of the egg carton and glue the remaining bowl to the middle of it to make a hat.

**5**

Paint the body white and the hat black.

**6**

Glue the hat in place. Tie a thin strip of felt around the neck for a scarf.

**7**

Add a little orange triangle for a carrot nose. Draw on some dots for eyes and a smile. Your super snowman is ready, come rain or shine!

**Handy Hint**

To make a circle, draw around a jar lid on cardstock.

BRRRR

# Mushrooms

## You will need

Two egg cartons
White and red paint

**1**

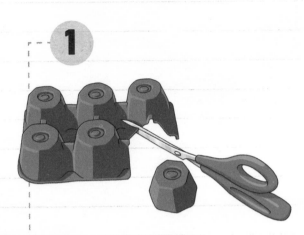

Cut the bowls from the base of an egg carton.

**2**

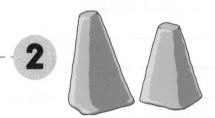

Cut out the pointed parts from the base of another egg carton.

**3**

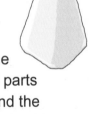

Paint the pointed parts white and the bowls red, with white spots.

**4**

Glue the bowls to the pointed parts. Arrange them to make a pretty woodland scene.

# Sheep

**Make one sheep
or a whole flock!**

## You will need

| | |
|---|---|
| Three egg cartons | Thick cardstock |
| White and black paint | Pink felt |
| | Two googly eyes |

**1**

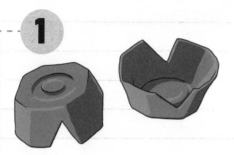

Cut four bowls from the base of an egg carton. Cut V-shaped notches into the sides of the bowls.

**2**

Glue the bowls to both sides of an upside-down egg carton, as shown. Paint it white.

**3**

Cut four bowls from the base of another egg carton for the feet. Paint them black.

**4**

Cut out a head from thick cardstock, and paint black.

**5**

Glue the head and legs into position. Add a pink nose, some googly eyes and a cute smile to finish your sheep.

BAA

# Bird Mask

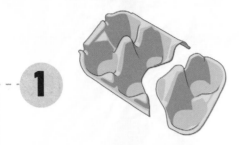

**You will need**

One egg carton

Brown and yellow paint

White felt

Elastic string

**1** Cut the end section from the base of an egg carton.

**2** To make eyes, press a pencil into the egg carton, as shown. Trim any rough edges.

**3** Turn over the carton, then cut a slit in the beak. Paint the head brown and the beak yellow.

**4** From felt, cut out two feathery eyebrows.

**5** Glue the eyebrows in place.

**6** With a pencil, make small holes on both sides of the beak. Thread a piece of elastic string through the holes. Tie a knot at each end to hold it in position. Your mask is ready.

# Bracelet

You could make this lovely bracelet for yourself or give it to a friend as a pretty present.

## You will need

**One egg carton**
**Pink paint**
**Yellow tissue paper**
**Ribbon**

**1** Cut three bowls from the base of an egg carton.

**2** Paint the bowls. Cut slits around the edges.

**3** Scrunch up some yellow tissue paper and glue it into the center of the bowls.

**4** Cut a piece of ribbon that is long enough to tie around your wrist. Glue it to the back of the flowers.

**5** Your bracelet is ready. Tie it around your wrist and finish with a pretty bow.

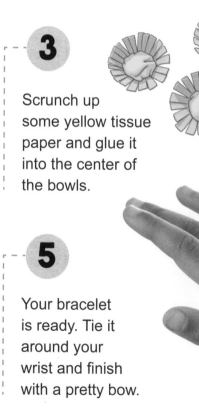

# Octopus

Turn your bedroom into a watery wonderland by making this cute and colorful octopus.

**1**

Cut two bowls from the base of an egg carton.

**2**

Glue the bowls to the top of an egg carton, for the eyes.

**3**

Cut the bottom discs from the other egg cartons, for the suckers.

**4**

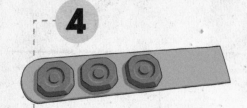

Cut out eight legs from cardboard. Glue the suckers to the legs.

**5**

Paint the carton a bright color, and add some contrasting spots.

**6**

Paint the legs to match the body.

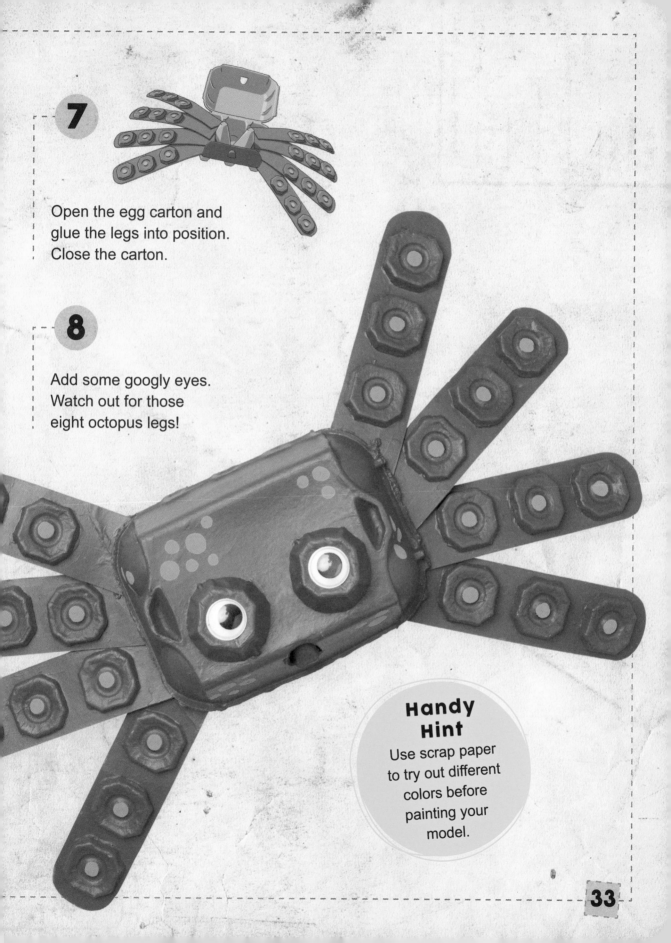

**7**

Open the egg carton and glue the legs into position. Close the carton.

**8**

Add some googly eyes. Watch out for those eight octopus legs!

**Handy Hint**

Use scrap paper to try out different colors before painting your model.

33

# Lovable Owl

Hoot, hoot! I can see you! Make this gorgeous little owl to watch over you all night long.

## You will need

Two egg cartons
Cardboard
Paint, including yellow paint
Two googly eyes

**1**

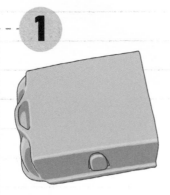

Cut the end from an egg carton.

**2**

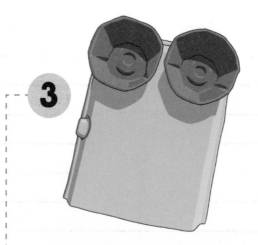

Cut two bowls from the base of another egg carton.

**3**

Glue the bowls to the front of the carton, for the owl's eyes.

**4**

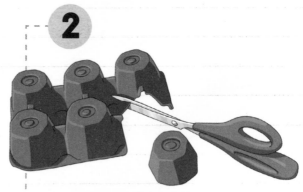

Paint the owl. Paint the eye sockets a contrasting color, so they really stand out.

**5**

Cut out two wings from the cardboard, and paint them to match the body.

**6**

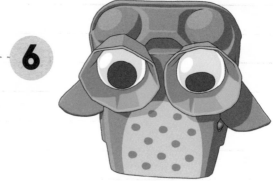

Glue the wings and googly eyes in place.

**7**

Cut out a cardstock triangle and paint it yellow. This is the beak. Fold it in half and glue in place. Your wise owl is ready to fly!

HOOT
HOOT

# Necklace

**You will need**

Two egg cartons    Ribbon
Paint    One bendy
Cardstock    straw

**1**

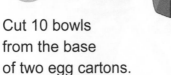

Cut 10 bowls
from the base
of two egg cartons.

**2**

Glue the bowls together to
make barrel-shaped beads.

**3**

Paint the beads.
Using a pencil, make
a hole from one end
of each bead to the other.

**4**

Glue a thin strip of cardstock
around the middle of each
bead. This will hide the joins.

**5**

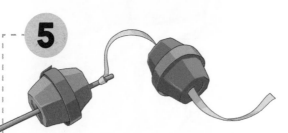

Cut a length of ribbon, attach it to a
straw, and thread it through the beads.

**6**

Tie the ends of the ribbon together.
Your pretty necklace is ready to wear.

# Bunny

**1**

Cut the end from an egg carton.

**2**

Cut out two long ears from cardstock.

**3**

Glue the ears to the top of the egg carton.

**4**

Cut two corners from the top of another egg carton. They will be feet.

**5**

Glue the feet in place. Paint your bunny.

**6**

Add a nose using a small piece of felt. Glue googly eyes onto two circles of felt to finish this frisky friend!

# Butterfly

**1**

Fold the paper in half and cut out a heart shape with a flat bottom, as shown. This will be your template.

**2**

Unfold the template. Draw around it on the cardboard and cut out.

**3**

Cut out a line of three bowls from the base of an egg carton.

**4**

Cut out the base of some egg carton bowls, to decorate the wings.

**5**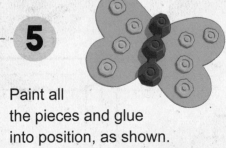

Paint all the pieces and glue into position, as shown.

**6**

Cut the bendy piece from two straws, and glue to the back of the head. Add some googly eyes. Glue a piece of ribbon to the back of the butterfly to hang it up.

# Caterpillar Pencil Holder

**1**

Cut the bowls from the base of an egg carton.

**2**

Glue two bowls together, to make a barrel. Make six barrels.

**3**

Paint the barrels bright colors. Cut a strip of cardboard, paint it green, and then glue your barrels onto it.

**4**

Use a pencil to make a hole in the top of five barrels. Leave the end barrel.

**5**

Make two small holes in the top of the end barrel. Insert two pieces of bendy straw. Glue googly eyes onto circles of felt, and add a smile. Place your pencils in the holes—your pencil holder is ready!

# Flower Garland

**1**

Cut the pointed parts from the bottom of an egg carton.

**2**

Cut a slit in each corner of the pointed parts. Bend the four corners outward.

**3**

Cut the edges into a petal shape. Paint them and leave to dry. Glue one pointed part onto another to make a flower. Repeat steps 1 to 3 to make as many flowers as you like.

**4**

Make a small hole in the middle of a flower. Thread through a piece of string.

**5**

Tie a knot in the string, as shown, then thread on your next flower.

**6**

Repeat step 5 until you have threaded on all your flowers. Tie a knot under the last flower. Decorate your bedroom with your beautiful flower garland.

# Snails

**Blaze a trail with these snails—
all your friends will want one!**

**1**

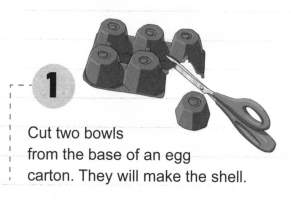

Cut two bowls from the base of an egg carton. They will make the shell.

**2**

Cut out a long triangle from cardboard. This will be the body. Paint the body and the shell pieces.

**3**

Glue the shell pieces onto either side of the body. Hold in place with a rubber band until dry.

**4**

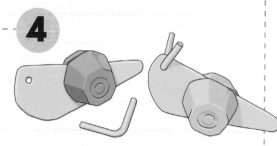

Cut a straw so the bendy part is in the middle. Make a hole in the body with a pencil. Insert the straw and bend upward.

**5**

Repeat steps 1 to 4 to make another snail. Add spots or stripes to the shell, googly eyes, and a smile. Why not make a set and line them up!

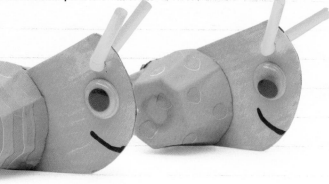

# Flower Wreath

This beautiful flower wreath will brighten up a dull, rainy day and add some springtime color to your home.

**1**

Draw a large circle onto a piece of cardboard. Draw a smaller circle inside. Cut out the large circle. Use a pencil to make a hole for your scissors, then cut out the middle circle to make a ring. Paint it green.

**2**

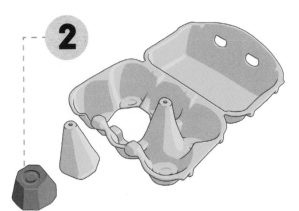

Cut the bowls and pointed parts from the bottom of the egg cartons.

**3**

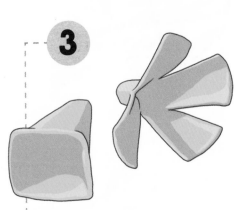

Cut a slit in each corner of the pointed parts. Bend the four corners outward.

**4**

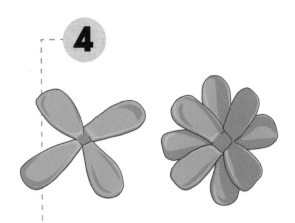

Cut the edges into a petal shape. Paint them. When they are dry, glue one pointed part onto another.

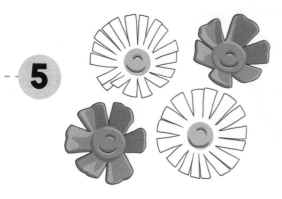

**5**

To make other types of flower, cut slits along the sides of the bowls, either close together or far apart, and bend outward. Paint lots of different colors.

**6**

Cut some leaves from the cardboard and paint them green. When the leaves and flowers are all dry, glue your flowers onto the ring.

**7**

Scrunch up some small pieces of tissue paper and glue in the centers of the flowers. Glue a piece of ribbon to the back of the garland. Find a spot in your home to hang your flower wreath —why not try one on your bedroom door?

# Fox Mask

**Be cleverly crafty and make this super-smart fox mask!**

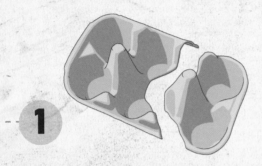

**1**

Cut the end section from the base of an egg carton, as shown.

**2**

To make the eyes, press a pencil into the egg carton, as shown. Trim any rough edges.

**3**

Turn over the carton. Paint the top part orange, and the bottom part white. Add a black nose.

**4**

Cut out two ears from cardstock, and paint them as shown. Glue the ears in place.

**5**

Make small holes on both sides of the nose with a pencil. Thread elastic string through the holes. Tie a knot at each end to hold it in position.

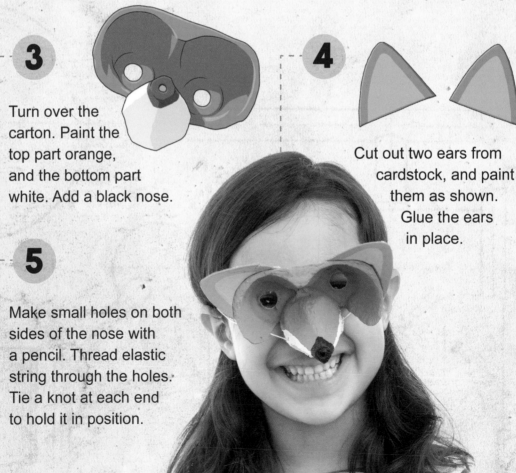

44

# Cute Noses

**1** Cut the bowls and the pointed parts from the base of an egg carton.

**2** Use a pointed part to make a beak. Cut a slit in it and paint yellow.

**3** You can make a piglet's nose from a bowl. Paint it pink and add some nostrils. A mouse's nose is made from a pointed part. Paint it gray, with a black tip. Add some thin strips of black cardstock for the whiskers.

**4** Make small holes with a pencil on both sides of each nose. Tie a length of elastic string to each nose and they are ready to wear! Which one do you like best?

# Penguins

These penguins will look adorable in your bathroom!

## You will need

**Two egg cartons**

**White, black, and pale blue paint**

**Yellow cardstock**

**Six googly eyes**

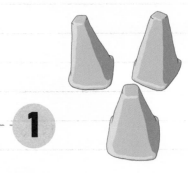

**1**

Cut three pointed parts from the base of an egg carton.

**2**

Paint on a white belly.

**3**

Paint the rest of the body black.

**4**

For the beak, cut out a triangle from a folded piece of yellow cardstock. Glue in place.

**5**

Paint the base of an egg carton to look like ice—your cute penguins can sit on it!

# Pink Piglet

## You will need

**Two egg cartons**
**Cardstock**
**Light pink, dark pink, and blue paint**
**Two googly eyes**

**1**

Cut off the end of an egg carton. This will be the piglet's body.

**2**

Cut out one bowl and two pointed parts from the base of another egg carton.

**3**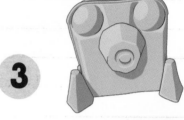

Glue a bowl to the front of the body. This is the snout. Glue the two pointed parts to the sides, to make the legs. Cut out two triangles from cardstock, for ears. Glue in place.

**4**

Paint the piglet pink. Paint the nose and feet darker pink.

**5**

Cut a strip of cardstock and paint it light pink. Wrap it around a pencil, to make a curly tail.

**6**

Glue the tail in place. Cut out two circles from the cardstock and paint them blue. Add them and the googly eyes to the piglet, as shown.

OINK OINK

# Robot

Robots at the ready! Make lots of these robots and you could create your own robot army!

**1**

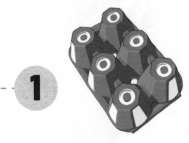

Paint an egg carton blue. Add white, as shown, to make it look metallic. This is the body.

**2**

Cut four pointed parts from the bottom of another egg carton. Paint them different colors.

**3**

Cut another egg carton in half. Paint it light blue. This will be the head. Glue the head to the top of the body.

**4**

Cut the bowls from the base of another egg carton. Glue two bowls together to make a barrel. Glue two barrels together to make two arms.

**5**

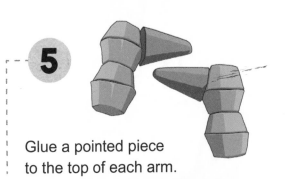

Glue a pointed piece to the top of each arm.

**6**

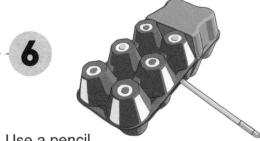

Use a pencil to make holes on both sides of the body, for the arms. Make two holes in the bottom, for the legs.

## 7

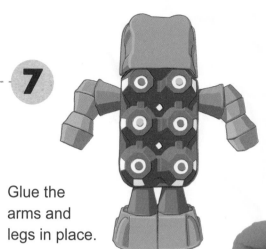

Glue the arms and legs in place.

## 8

Glue two bowls to the head and add some googly eyes. Cut a strip of cardstock for the mouth, and glue on.

## 9

Cut the ends off the top of an egg carton, and paint. Recycle the middle bit. Glue it to the bottom of the legs.

### Handy Hint

Always allow the glue to dry completely before moving your model.

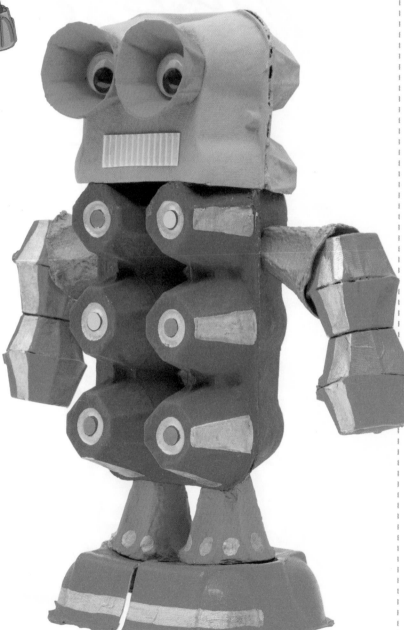

# Rocket

5, 4, 3, 2, 1 ... Get ready for blast-off with this bright rocket.

**You will need**

Three egg cartons
Paint, including red and blue

**1**

Cut two pointed parts from the base of an egg carton. Paint them red. Paint another egg carton blue.

**2**

Use a pencil to make two holes in the end of the egg carton. Insert the pointed parts and glue into position.

**3**

Cut off the corner of another egg carton, to make a triangle.

**4**

Glue the triangle to the top of the egg carton, and paint blue. Paint on some details, including windows, and your cool rocket is ready to go!

WHOOSH

# Spider

**1**

Paint the bottom part of an egg carton black.

**2**

Cut out eight legs from cardstock, and paint black.

**3**

Bend each leg into a Z shape.

**4**

Glue the legs to the underside of the body.

**5**

Turn over the spider, and paint on some pink spots. Cut out circles from the cardstock and paint them pink. Add them and the googly eyes, and find someone to scare!

51

# Spotty Snake

Sssssssssssssssssssssss! This sensationally spotty snake is ssssso stunning you will want to make more than just one!

**1** Cut the bowls from the base of the egg cartons. The more bowls you cut, the longer your snake will be.

**2** Place two bowls together to make a barrel. Use all the bowls you cut to make lots of barrels.

**3** Paint the barrels bright colors. Use a pencil to make holes through both ends of the barrels.

**4** Cut a pointed part from the base of an egg carton. Paint it, and make a hole in the small end with a pencil.

**5**

Tie a knot in a long piece of string. Attach the string to a straw, then thread through all the barrels. Tie a knot in the end of the string.

sssss

**6**

Cut a strip of red cardstock. Cut a V in one end. This will be the tongue. Glue in place and add googly eyes. Your snake is ready to slither!

**Handy Hint**
Paint spots onto the barrels to make your snake really stand out.

# Kangaroo

## You will need

**Three egg cartons**
**Cardboard**
**Light and dark brown, cream, and pink paint**
**Four googly eyes**
**Green felt**

**1**

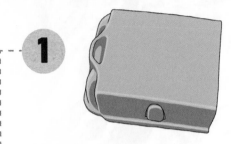

Cut off the end of an egg carton.

**2**

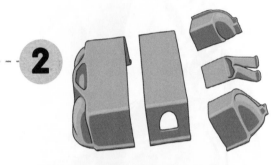

Cut the lid of another egg carton into sections, as shown. The large piece will be a pouch. The small pieces will be feet.

**3**

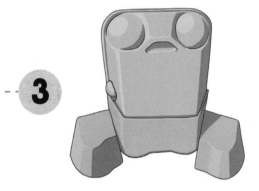

Glue the pouch to the front of the egg carton. Glue the feet to the sides of the egg carton, as shown.

**4**

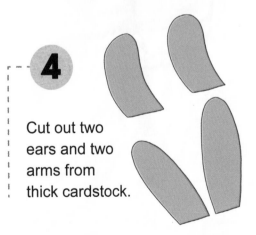

Cut out two ears and two arms from thick cardstock.

**5**

Glue the ears and arms into position. Paint the body light brown, with a cream belly. Add some pink to the ears.

## 6

Cut a bowl from the base of an egg carton. Cut out two small ears from cardboard. Paint dark brown and pink.

## 7

Glue the baby kangaroo into the mother's pouch. Add a pair of cardstock arms, as shown.

## 8

For the mother, place the googly eyes onto circles of green felt and glue into position. Glue the baby's eyes on too. Add noses and smiles.

### Handy Hint
Not all kangaroos are reddish-brown, some are gray, so you could use gray paint, too.

# Mustache Mask

No one will recognize you
with this great disguise!

## You will need

One egg carton

Pink and
black paint

Cardboard

Elastic string

**1** Cut the end from the base
of an egg carton, as shown.

**2** To make eyes, press a pencil
into the egg carton, as shown.
Trim any rough edges.

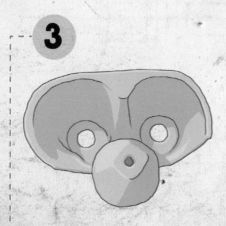

**3** Paint your
mask pink.

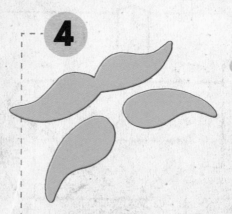

**4** From cardboard,
cut out a mustache
and a pair of eyebrows.
Paint them black.

**5**

Glue the
mustache and
eyebrows in place.

**6**

On either side of the nose,
make a hole with a pencil.
Thread a piece of elastic string
through the holes. Tie a knot at
each end to hold it in position.
Now your disguise is ready!

TA DAH!

# Mini Bugs

## You will need

**One egg carton**
**Paint**
**Black felt or cardstock**
**Six googly eyes**

**1**

Cut three bowls from the base of an egg carton.

**Handy Hint**
In nature, the brighter the colors, the deadlier the bug!

**2**

Paint the bowls bright colors.

**3**

Add spots or stripes.

**4**

Cut 18 narrow strips of black felt or cardstock. Glue six to the inside of each bowl.

**5**

Add a pair of googly eyes to each bug and they're ready to scuttle away!

# Pretty Fish

Turn your bedroom or bathroom into a sea world adventure zone with this pretty fish display.

## You will need

**Three egg cartons**
**Paint**
**Four straws**
**Ten googly eyes**

**1**

Make five fish. For each, cut three bowls from an egg carton.

**2**

Glue two of the bowls together, to make a barrel. Glue the other bowl to the top, to make the tail.

**3**

Cut a V-shaped notch in each tail. Paint the inside and outside different colors. Add some spots or stripes, a dot for a mouth, and googly eyes.

**4**

Use a pencil to make a hole in the bottom of each fish. Insert the straws into the holes, and glue into position.

**5**

Paint the lid of an egg carton and make some holes with a pencil. Insert the straws into the holes, and glue them into position.

# Duckling

## You will need

**One egg carton**
**Yellow paint**
**Orange cardstock**
**Two googly eyes**

**1**

Cut three bowls and one pointed part from the base of an egg carton.

**2**

Glue the two bowls together, to make a barrel. Then glue the pointed part to the top.

**3**

Glue the other bowl onto the pointed part. Paint all parts yellow.

**4**

Cut out two webbed feet and a bill from a piece of orange cardstock. Glue the feet and bill into position.

**5**

Add two googly eyes and your duck is ready to quack, quack, quack!

# Mouse Finger Puppet

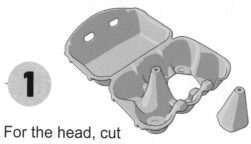

**1** For the head, cut a pointed part from the base of an egg carton.

**2** Paint the part gray or white. Paint the end black.

**3** Cut out two ears from cardstock. Paint them to match the head.

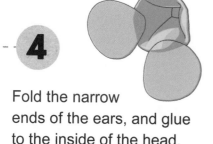

**4** Fold the narrow ends of the ears, and glue to the inside of the head.

**5** Paint the inside of the ears pink, and add a pair of googly eyes. Squeak!

# Goggle Eyes

**Amaze your friends with these incredible goggle eyes!**

## You will need

One egg carton
Paint
Black cardstock
Elastic string

**1** Cut two bowls from the base of an egg carton.

**2** Use a pencil to make a hole in the center of the bowls. Trim any rough edges.

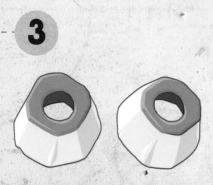

**3** Paint the sides of the bowls white and the tops any eye color you choose.

**4** Cut two strips of black card. Cut slits along one edge. Glue to the tops of the bowls, for eyelashes.

**5**

Make small holes on both sides of the bowls. Thread a short piece of elastic string through the middle holes, as shown. Tie a knot at each end. Repeat using a longer piece of elastic string for the other two holes on the outer edge. Your goggle eyes are ready to wear.

**Handy Hint**

You can add extra eyelashes to the bottom of your eyes, too!

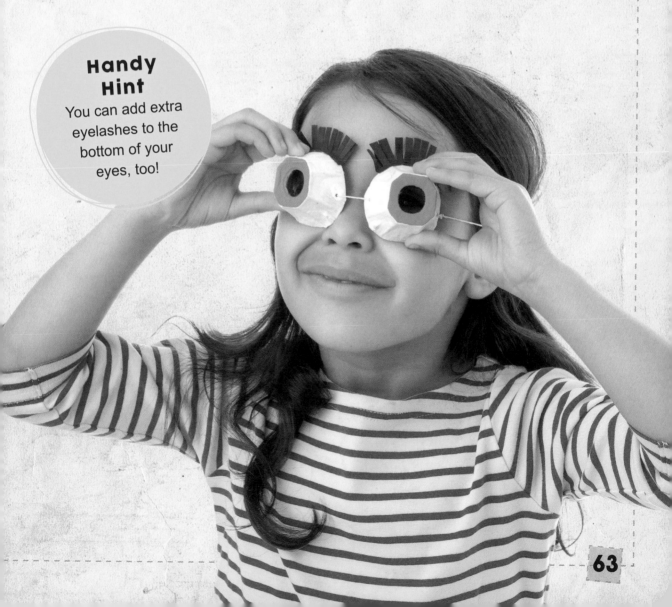

# Monster

Are there monsters in your bedroom? Scare them off with this happy little monster friend!

## You will need

**Three egg cartons**
**Paint**
**Three googly eyes**

**1**

Cut a row of three bowls from the base of an egg carton.

**2**

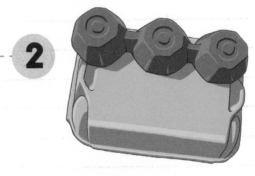

Glue the bowls onto another egg carton to make the monster's body.

**3**

To make the feet, cut both ends off the lid of an egg carton.

**4**

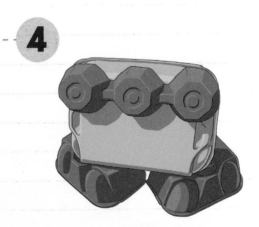

Glue the ends to the base of the monster's body.

**5**

Cut two pointed parts from the base of an egg carton, for the horns. Paint the monster.

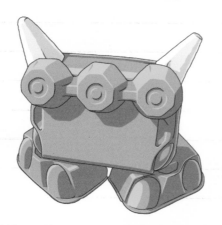

**6**

Paint on spots and claws, and three circles of pink. Glue googly eyes on top. Add a smile to this not-so-scary monster!

SO CUTE!

# Crocodile

This snappy croc will keep guard outside your bedroom. Why not make another crocodile and let them snap at each other?

**1**

Cut two bowls from the bottom of an egg carton for the eyes.

**2**

Cut about five pointed parts from the bottom of another egg carton, for the spiky tail. Cut them into different sizes.

**3**

Place the short-side opening egg carton upright, with another regular carton next to it, upside-down. Arrange the tail spikes in a line, as shown. Cut a piece of cardboard the same length as the crocodile.

**4**

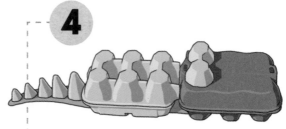

Glue all the parts onto the cardboard. Glue the eye pieces to the top of the head.

**5**

Paint the crocodile a bright green, with yellow spots. Add googly eyes.

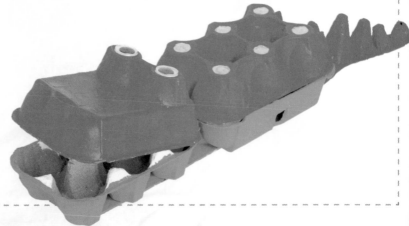

# Witch

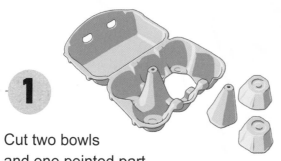

**1** Cut two bowls and one pointed part from the base of an egg carton.

**2** Glue the two bowls together, to make a barrel. Paint all the parts black.

**3** Paint a foam ball yellow. Glue to the top of the barrel.

**4** Cut a strip of purple felt. Make slits along one edge. Glue to the inside of the hat.

**5** Cut a cape from some black felt and glue it to the body.

**6** Draw on some features and make a pumpkin. You will need another barrel, orange paint, a green straw, and felt.

# Pirate Ship

Ahoy there, me hearties!
Prepare to set sail on the
seven seas with this awesome
pirate ship—arrrrgh!

## You will need

**Two 12-egg cartons**

**One six-egg carton**

**Brown, blue, black,
and red paint**

**Yellow and white
cardstock**

**Three straws**

**1**

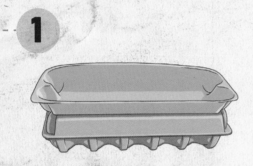

Glue the top of a long egg carton
onto another long egg carton.

**2**

Glue a small egg carton onto
the top. Paint all cartons brown.

**3**

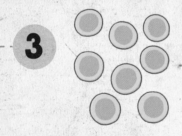

Cut out lots of yellow circles.
Paint the middles pale blue.
These will be the portholes.

**4**

Glue the portholes into position.

**5**

From cardstock, cut out five different-
sized squares. Paint one with stripes
and another with a skull and crossbones.
These will be the ship's sails.

**6**

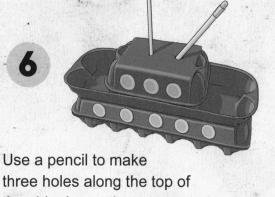

Use a pencil to make three holes along the top of the ship. Insert three straws into the holes for the masts, and glue into position.

**7**

Glue the sails to the straws before setting off on your next pirate adventure.

LAND AHOY!

**Handy Hint**
You can add some colored cardstock to make the ship's deck, too.

# Plane

You could make lots of these cool little planes and hang them from your bedroom ceiling.

## You will need

Two egg cartons
Paint, including blue
Cardboard, including yellow
Metal fastener

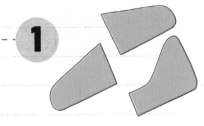

**1** Cut out two wings and a tail from cardboard.

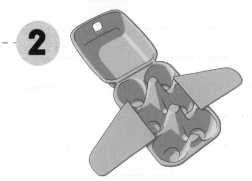

**2** Glue the wings to the inside of an opened egg carton.

**3** Cut a slit in one end of the carton, and glue the tail into position. Paint your plane.

**4** Cut a bowl from another egg carton, cut a notch in either side, and paint the same color as your plane. Cut a pointed part from the egg carton. Cut four slits, flatten the part, and paint a different color. This will be the propeller for your plane.

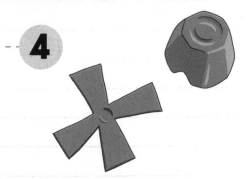

**5** Make a hole with pencil in the middle of the propeller and the bowl. Use a metal fastener to attach them, as shown.

**6**

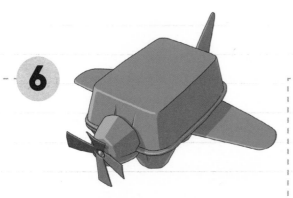

Glue the nose and
propeller into position.

**7**

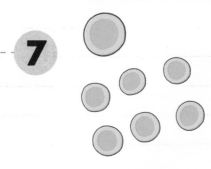

Cut out six small yellow circles
and a large one. Paint the
centers pale blue. Cut the large
circle in half, to make windows
for the front of the plane.

**8**

Glue the windows into position.

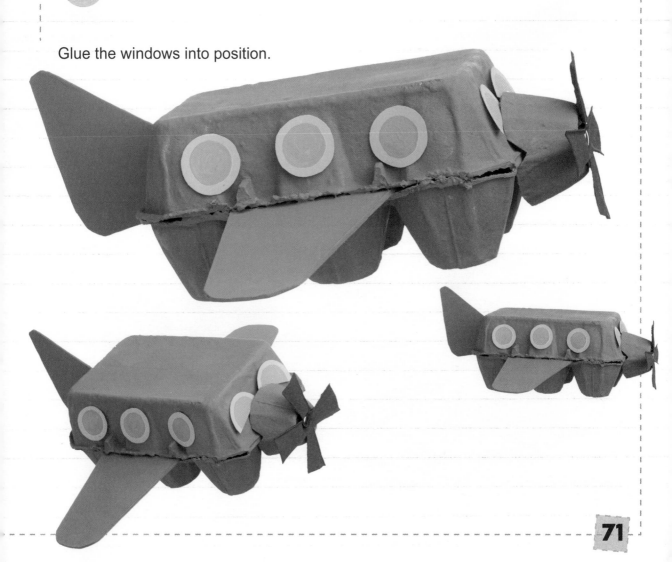

# Treasure Chest

Nowhere to hide your lovely loot? Problem solved. Make this awesome treasure chest, then hide all your booty in it!

## You will need

Three egg cartons
Brown and yellow paint
Yellow cardstock
Ribbon for the treasure

**1**

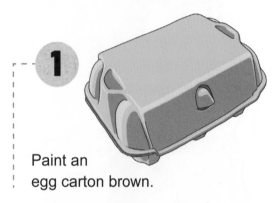

Paint an egg carton brown.

**2**

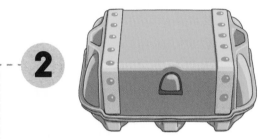

Cut two strips of yellow cardstock and glue to the top of the carton. Draw on some rivets with an orange pen.

**3**

Fold a piece of yellow cardstock in half, and cut out a padlock, as shown.

**4**

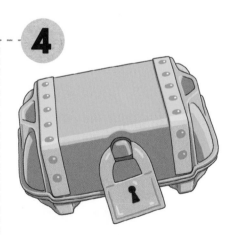

Draw on the keyhole with a black pen.

**5**

Cut out circles from the bases of two more egg cartons. Glue them to the ribbon to make treasure, and paint yellow.

**6**

You can make necklaces and gold, too. Keep it hidden from any pirates, though!

# Tugboat

This tugboat is so simple to make, you could make lots of them—and have plenty of time to play with them afterward.

## You will need

One 12-egg carton
Two six-egg cartons
Paint
Yellow and gray cardstock

**1**

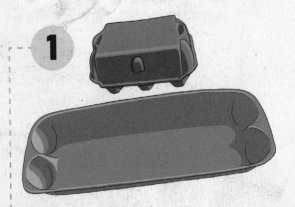

Cut the top off a long egg carton, and paint it. Paint a small egg carton a different color.

**2**

Glue the small egg carton onto the middle of the long carton.

**3**

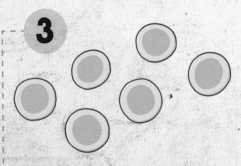

Cut out lots of yellow circles. Paint the centers pale blue. These will be the portholes.

CHUG CHUG

**4**

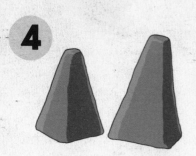

Cut two pointed parts from the base of an egg carton, and paint. These will be the funnels.

**5**

Use a pencil to make two holes along the top of the boat. Insert the funnels and glue into position.

**6**

Cut out a cloud shape from gray cardstock. Make a slit in the bottom, and slot onto one of funnels, for billowing smoke. Your tugboat is now ready to go to work!

# Tractor

Vroom, beep, beep! Life on a farm is busy, so get ready to make this hard-working tractor, then put it to work!

## You will need

**Three egg cartons**

**Red, white, black, and blue paint**

**Cardboard**

**Shiny corrugated cardstock**

**1**

Cut two lids from egg cartons, and glue together to make the body of the tractor.

**2**

Cut another carton in half and glue the bottom edges together to make the cab.

**3**

Cut a V-shaped notch in the bottom of the cab.

**4**

Glue the cab to the body, as shown, and paint them red.

**5**

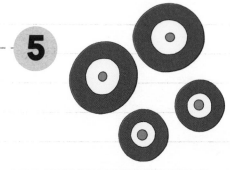

Cut out two large and two small circles from cardboard. Paint them to look like wheels.

**6**

Glue the wheels to the tractor body.

**7**

Add some windows and a shiny grille made from corrugated cardstock so your tractor can chug, chug along!

# Cute Crab

This cheerful little crab will look cute in a bathroom or with other sea creatures.

## You will need

**Two egg cartons**
**Cardstock**
**Paint**
**Two metal fasteners**
**Two googly eyes**

**1** Cut two bowls from the base of an egg carton.

**2** Glue the bowls to the top of another carton, for the eyes.

**3** From cardstock, cut two claws. Make sure they are large enough to fit around your crab's body, as shown.

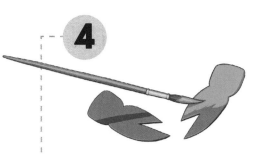

**4** Now paint the claws.

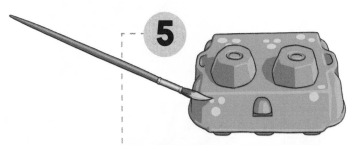

**5** Paint the crab's body, and add some spots to its shell.

**6**

Use a pencil to push a hole through the claw and shell of the crab. Attach each claw to the body with a metal fastener.

**Handy Hint**

Make the holes in step 6 smaller than the head of the metal fastener.

**7**

Add some googly eyes. Your crab is now ready, but be careful it doesn't pinch you!

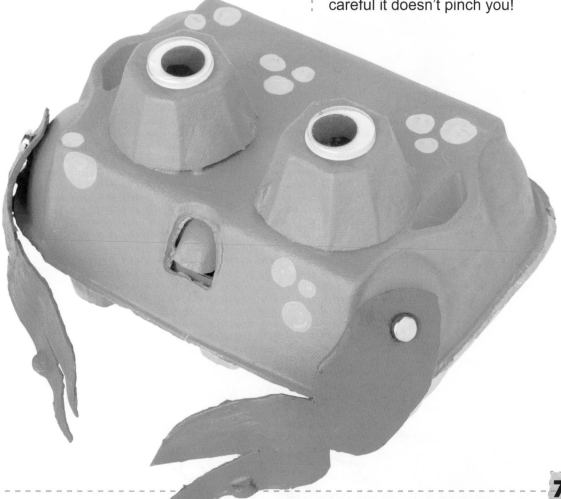

Quarto is the authority on a wide range of topics.

Quarto educates, entertains and enriches the lives of our readers—enthusiasts and lovers of hands-on living.

www.quartoknows.com

Publisher: Maxime Boucknooghe
Editorial Director: Victoria Garrard
Art Director: Miranda Snow
Editors: Sophie Hallam, Sarah Eason and Jennifer Sanderson
Designer: Paul Myerscough
Photographer: Michael Wicks
Illustrator: Tom Connell
With thanks to our wonderful models Islah, Ethan, and Ania.

First published in the United States in 2016
by QEB Publishing, Inc.
Part of The Quarto Group
6 Orchard
Lake Forest, CA 92630

A CIP record for this book is available from the Library of Congress.

ISBN  978 1 68297 004 1

Printed in China